For the children.

Jesus said,
"Let the little children come to me, and do
not hinder them, for the kingdom of heaven
belongs to such as these."

Matthew 19 v 14

"A sweet, winsome way to point children to the Lord while giving them tangible help in calming strong emotions."
JULIE LOWE, Counselor and Faculty at CCEF, author of *Building Bridges: Biblical Counseling Activities for Children and Teens*

"I wholeheartedly commend Eliza Huie to you, and specifically this biblically focused, practically effective book that will help children to cast their cares on God."
DAVID PLATT, Lead Pastor at McLean Bible Church

"This wonderful little book acknowledges children's strong emotions and helpfully gives a model that takes the child (and adult) to our heavenly Father."
JANE WATKINS, Director of Mentoring at Growing Young Disciples

"A wonderfully practical, engaging, and biblical book that we wish we had had ten years ago."
JEFF AND SARAH WALTON, Authors of *Together Through the Storms*

"Kids have big feelings. This beautiful book will train your family to bring their emotions—their hearts—to God. I strongly recommend it."
JARED KENNEDY, Editor at The Gospel Coalition; Author of *The Beginner's Gospel Story Bible*

"Eliza Huie has done a tremendous job in empowering kids to process their feelings in positive ways and offering a foundation of faith for when those feelings try to take over. I'm thrilled for myself, as a therapist, and for the world to have this helpful and heartwarming resource."
SISSY GOFF, Director of Child and Adolescent Counseling at Daystar Counseling; Author of *Raising Worry-Free Girls*

"A brilliant, God-focused breathing exercise to help children deal with their emotions."
BOB HARTMAN, Author of *The Prisoners, the Earthquake, and the Midnight Song*

"A wonderful children's resource for troubled hearts, which gives parents practical strategies for helping children focus on what brings lasting peace—our good and gracious God."
CHAMP THORNTON, Author of *The Radical Book for Kids* and *Why Do We Say Thank You?*

Count Yourself Calm
© Eliza Huie 2023

Illustrated by Mike Henson | Design & Art Direction by André Parker

"The Good Book For Children" is an imprint of The Good Book Company Ltd
thegoodbook.com | thegoodbook.co.uk | thegoodbook.com.au
thegoodbook.co.nz | thegoodbook.co.in

ISBN: 9781784988135 | Printed in India

Count Yourself Calm

Written by
Eliza Huie

Illustrated by
Mike Henson

Have you ever had a bad day?

A day when things are not ok and your feelings
are so big that it's hard to breathe?

Those days can feel like **EVERYTHING** is going wrong, and **NOTHING** seems to make it better.

Maybe you feel sad.

Or maybe you are angry.

Perhaps you're feeling worried...

... lonely, scared, or hurt.

Did you know that everyone has days like that?

Your friends do.

Your teachers do.

Your parents do.

Your grandparents
do too.

Even people in the Bible had times
when everything felt really, really bad.

On days like that, there is a little activity that can be a big help.

We can learn it on the good days and practice it on the hard days. It is as easy as counting down from five and will help to steady your heart and your mind.

It starts with a breath and a prayer...

Let's take a breath together.

Before you breathe, gently cross your arms over your chest. Imagine your lungs are balloons and you need to fill them all the way up with air. Breathe in through your nose and feel your arms go up with your breath.

Now, slowly let the air out of your lungs through your mouth and imagine the balloons deflating.

How did that feel?

Let's do it again. This time, as you breathe in, say this prayer:

"God, help me trust you..."

... and as you breathe out, pray,

"... with all my heart" (Proverbs 3 v 5).

Next, we count down.

As we count down from five, we are going to stop to notice things. Noticing things means we pay attention to them. We make our minds think about them. As our minds think about these things, our bodies and emotions will join in.

5

Can you name **FIVE** things God made that bring you joy?

God's word says, "The LORD has done great things for us, and we are filled with joy" (Psalm 126 v 3).

4 Now list **FOUR** gifts from God that make you feel peaceful.

God's word says, "In peace I will lie down and sleep, for you alone, LORD, make me dwell in safety" (Psalm 4 v 8).

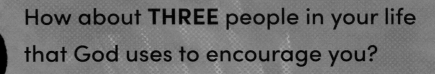

3 How about **THREE** people in your life that God uses to encourage you?

God's word says, "Encourage one another and build each other up" (1 Thessalonians 5 v 11).

2 Share **TWO** promises of
God that give you hope.

God's word says, "May the God of hope fill you with all joy and peace as you trust in him, so that you may overflow with hope" (Romans 15 v 13).

1

What is **ONE** word that describes God and calms you down?

God's word says, "God is our refuge and strength, a helper who is always found in times of trouble" (Psalm 46 v 1, CSB).

You did it!
Now, let's end where we began,
with a breath and a prayer.

Before we take another deep
breath together, gently cross your
arms over your chest once again.

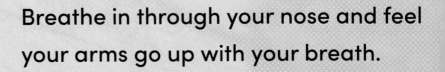

Think of your lungs as those big balloons
that you will fill all the way up with air.

Breathe in through your nose and feel
your arms go up with your breath.

Now, slowly let the air out of your lungs through your mouth and imagine the balloons deflating.

Let's take one more breath, this time with a prayer. Take a deep breath in, and as you do, pray these words:

"God help me trust you..."
And as you breath out, pray,
"... with all my heart" (Proverbs 3 v 5).

How do you feel now?

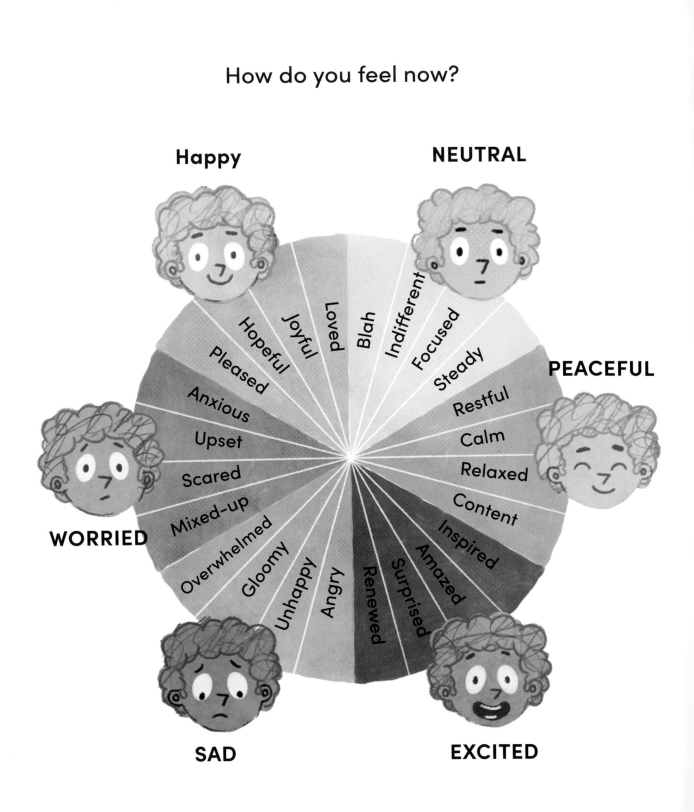

You don't have to wait for a bad day to practice this exercise. Come back to it as often as you like. The more you practice, the more it will come to mind on those days when things are not going well. It is as simple as remembering to count down from five and notice all the ways God helps you.

A Word To Parents

This is an adaptation of a calming activity that uses the five senses. In the original activity, children are encouraged to use the 5-4-3-2-1 countdown to focus on each of the five senses as a way to distract the child from a distressing situation. Instead of merely providing distraction, the five steps in this book help to focus the child's attention on the help that God brings to their life.

Reading this book with your child will familiarize them with this calming activity. It is best to read it when the child is not in distress. Practice it with the child as you read. In time, what was read and practiced can then be called to mind whenever your child needs help calming down. Whether you are reading the book or recalling what it has shared in a moment of struggle, always start by taking a deep breath with the child and saying a brief prayer together. As you breathe, ask God for help as you do the activity. Then simply walk your child through each of the five steps, giving plenty of time for them to respond. Once you have gone through the five steps, take another deep breath and pray again, with the child thanking God for the help he provides.